Weather Update

Droughts

by Nathan Olson

Consultant:
Joseph M. Moran, PhD
Associate Director, Education Program
American Meteorological Society
Washington, D.C.

Mankato, Minnesota

Bridgestone Books are published by Capstone Press,
151 Good Counsel Drive, P.O. Box 669, Mankato, Minnesota 56002.
www.capstonepress.com

Printed in the United States of America

Library of Congress Cataloging-in-Publication Data
Olson, Nathan.
Droughts / by Nathan Olson.
p. cm.—(Bridgestone books. Weather update)
Includes bibliographical references (p. 23) and index.
Summary: "A brief introduction to droughts, including what they are, what they impact, and types of droughts"—Provided by publisher.
ISBN 0-7368-4331-0
1. Droughts—Juvenile literature. I. Title. II. Series.
QC929.25.O38 2006
551.57'73—dc22 2004029082

Editorial Credits
Jennifer Besel, editor; Molly Nei, set designer; Kate Opseth, book designer; Wanda Winch, photo researcher; Scott Thoms, photo editor

Photo Credits
Art Directors/Bob Turner, 10, 14; Helene Rogers, 8
Corbis, 20; Bill Ross, cover; Eric and David Hosking, 16
The Image Finders/Mark E. Gibson, 18
Photodisc/PhotoLink, 6
Tom Pantages, 12
Visuals Unlimited/Inga Spence, 4; Theo Allofs, 1

1 2 3 4 5 6 10 09 08 07 06 05

Table of Contents

What Is a Drought? 5
Types of Drought 7
Where Droughts Happen 9
Prevailing Winds 11
Forecasting Droughts 13
Measuring Droughts 15
The Impact of Droughts 17
Wildfires and Dust Storms 19
Major Droughts in History 21
Glossary 22
Read More 23
Internet Sites 23
Index 24

What Is a Drought?

A farmer looks out at his field. The crops are brown. The ground is cracked. Rain has not fallen in months. A drought has ruined the harvest.

A drought is a long period of dry weather. Little rain and high temperatures dry up the ground, plants, and lakes. Droughts can last for weeks, months, or years.

◀ A farmer looks at crops destroyed by drought.

Types of Drought

All droughts are caused by too little **precipitation**. Scientists talk about droughts by their impact, or type.

Three types of drought can affect an area. A place has a **meteorological** drought when it gets less rain than usual. **Agricultural** droughts cause crops to dry up and die. A **hydrological** drought dries up lakes and rivers. During a long drought, an area will feel the effects of all three types of drought.

Farmers try to save their crops by watering them during an agricultural drought.

Where Droughts Happen

Droughts can happen anywhere. Some areas are hurt by droughts more often than others. Many droughts hit places near deserts. The Sahel (suh-HEEL) is a grassland near the Sahara desert in North Africa. Droughts in the Sahel last for many years.

In North America, the **Great Plains** has many droughts. Much of the United States' food is grown in the Great Plains. Droughts damage crops and hurt farm animals. People have less food to eat.

◀ People and animals in the Sahel have trouble finding food to eat during long droughts.

Prevailing Winds

Every area has prevailing, or usual, wind patterns. If these winds change, the weather changes, too. A change in the winds can sometimes push rainstorms away. The lack of rain causes a drought.

Winds can also stop clouds from forming. Clouds form when wet, warm air is pushed upward to cool. When the winds change, the air sinks toward the ground. The water in the air doesn't cool. Clouds can't form. Without clouds, rain cannot fall.

A change in the prevailing winds pushes rain away. Grasses and trees dry up.

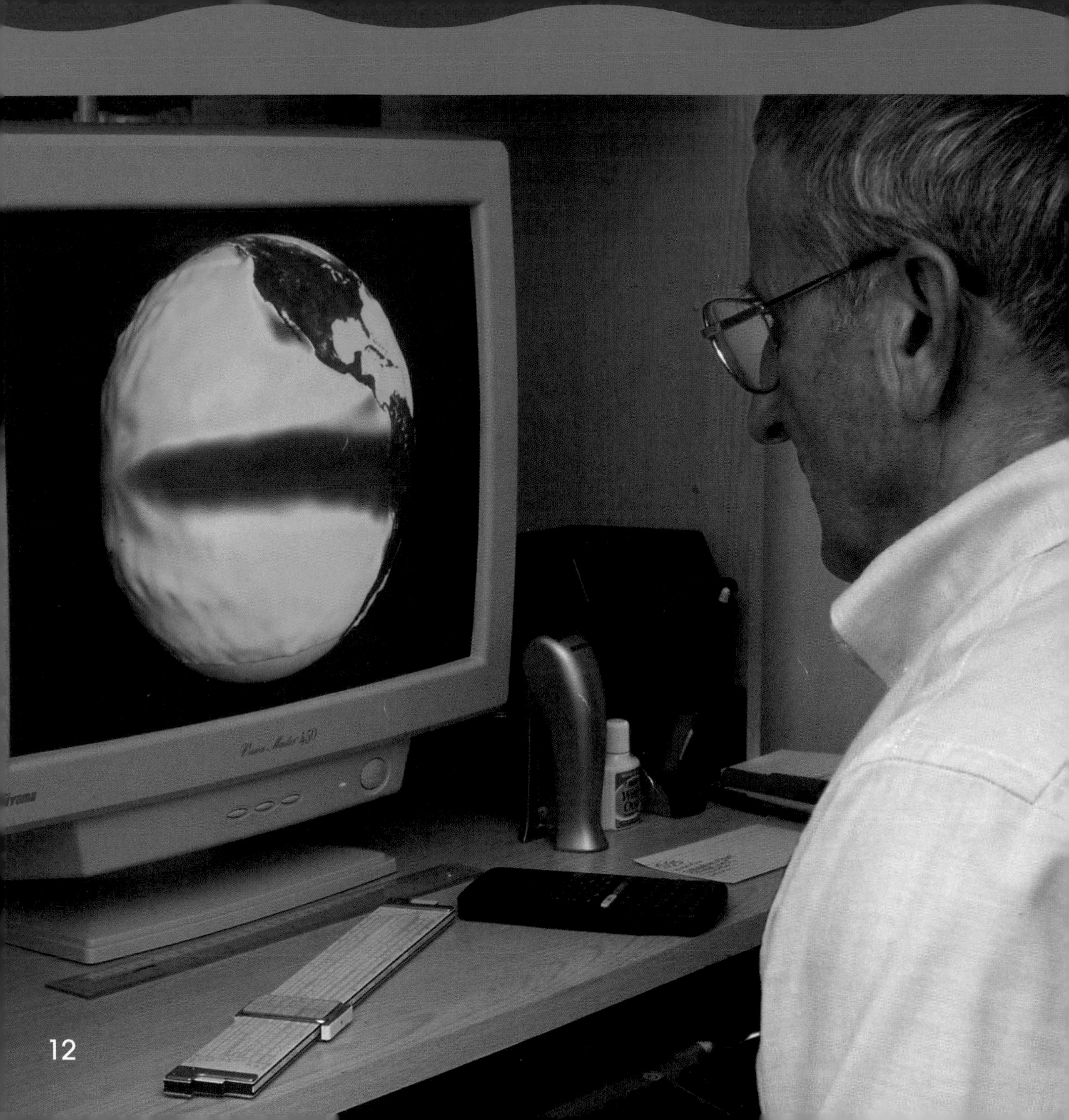

Forecasting Droughts

A drought is hard to **forecast**. Scientists have to watch for changes in the usual weather patterns.

A change in ocean water temperatures can change weather patterns around the world. El Niño (EL NEEN-yoh) happens when water temperatures in the Pacific Ocean near Peru get warmer than usual. El Niño may bring droughts to Asia and Australia. La Niña (LA NEEN-yah) happens when water temperatures get colder. La Niña may cause droughts in the southern United States.

◂ Scientists use computer images to watch the effects of El Niño and La Niña around the world.

Measuring Droughts

Measuring droughts is not easy. Scientists watch water supplies. Water comes into the supply from rain, snow, and groundwater. Then the water **evaporates** or is used by plants. When more water is used than is brought in, a drought will happen.

Scientists use the **Palmer Index** to study droughts. This index measures the water supply. A score of minus four on the index means a place is in a severe drought.

Droughts are even measured in deserts. Dry plants and cracks in the ground show this desert is drier than usual.

The Impact of Droughts

People, plants, and animals need water. During droughts, it can be hard to find clean water to drink. Sometimes the small amount of water left during a drought fills with **bacteria**. The bacteria are harmful to people and animals.

Without rain, plants will die. Hungry animals search the dry ground for food. Crops can't grow without water. People need these crops for food. During a severe drought, people and animals can starve.

◄ Birds and other animals can become ill when their water supply is dried up by a drought.

Wildfires and Dust Storms

During a drought, a bolt of lightning or a spark from a campfire can cause a wildfire. Dried-up plants and grasses burn easily. These fires can burn forests and grasslands. Wildfires can also kill animals.

Dust storms and dust devils are common during droughts. Dust storms happen when strong winds pick up dirt. The winds and dirt make a wall of dust. Dust devils are like tiny tornadoes. Spinning winds pick up dirt to form a funnel. Dust storms and dust devils can harm land and buildings.

◂ Dry grass catches fire easily. Grasses and trees burned during this wildfire in Mount Shasta, California.

Major Droughts in History

From 1931 to 1937, North America suffered through the Dust Bowl. This drought caused large dust storms to sweep across the Great Plains. As crops dried up, many farmers left the Great Plains to find new jobs.

China has had some of the world's worst droughts. From 1876 to 1879 at least 9 million people died because a drought left them with no food or water.

People have learned some ways to live through droughts. Still, droughts cause hunger and thirst around the world.

Huge clouds of dust rolled over the Great Plains during the Dust Bowl.

Glossary

agricultural (ag-ruh-KUL-chur-uhl)—to do with farming

bacteria (bak-TIHR-ee-uh)—tiny living things that are all around; some bacteria can cause illness.

evaporate (e-VAP-uh-rate)—to change from a liquid to a gas

forecast (FOR-kast)—to say what you think will happen to the weather

Great Plains (GRAYT PLANES)—the central part of North America; in the United States it includes Colorado, Kansas, Montana, Nebraska, New Mexico, North and South Dakota, Oklahoma, Texas, and Wyoming.

hydrological (hye-droh-LOJ-ik-uhl)—to do with water

meteorological (mee-tee-uh-roh-LAH-ji-kuhl)—to do with the study of weather

Palmer Index (PAL-mer IN-deks)—a chart used to measure the strength of a drought

precipitation (pri-sip-i-TAY-shuhn)—water that falls from clouds to the earth's surface

Read More

Spilsbury, Louise, and Richard Spilsbury. *Dreadful Droughts.* Awesome Forces of Nature. Chicago: Heinemann, 2003.

Ylvisaker, Anne. *Droughts.* Natural Disasters. Mankato, Minn.: Capstone High-Interest Books, 2003.

Internet Sites

FactHound offers a safe, fun way to find Internet sites related to this book. All of the sites on FactHound have been researched by our staff.

Here's how:
1. Visit *www.facthound.com*
2. Type in this special code **0736843310** for age-appropriate sites. Or enter a search word related to this book for a more general search.
3. Click on the **Fetch It** button.

FactHound will fetch the best sites for you!

Index

animals, 9, 17, 19

bacteria, 17

China, 21
clouds, 11, 21
crops, 5, 7, 9, 17, 21

deserts, 9, 15
Dust Bowl, 21
dust devils, 19
dust storms, 19, 21

El Niño, 13
evaporation, 15

farmers, 5, 7, 21

Great Plains, 9, 21

La Niña, 13

Palmer Index, 15
precipitation, 5, 7, 11, 15, 17

Sahel, 9
scientists, 7, 13, 15

temperatures, 5, 13
types of droughts, 7

wildfires, 19
winds, 11, 19